The Ford Motor Company Assembly Plant
Mahwah, NJ

1955 – 1980

Thomas O'Brien

Table of Contents

List of Illustrations

Acknowledgements

This project has been interesting and challenging. The Ford Assembly Plant was an important part of the history of Mahwah, NJ. Although I found that there was a significant amount of material available, I could find no documents that captured the complete story. This document is my attempt to compile an illustrated history of the Ford Motor Company Mahwah Assembly Plant and the effect it had on the area, the population, and the ongoing impact. It is a collection of facts, figures, articles, photos, internet sources, and personal interviews, brought together to tell the story of this impressive building and its workers.

This project would not have been possible without the guidance and assistance of several key people:

Tom Dunn, Charlie Carraras, and Marion Brown for their assistance in locating and providing access to the museum archives.

Robert Adler for sharing railroad diagrams and photos from his personal collections.

Joe Bogonian, an employee at the plant for thirteen years, for sharing his personal experiences and knowledge about the day-to-day operations.

Gail Doscher, who provided personal support and encouragement during the course of the project.

Bill LaForet for his video of the demolition of the Ford Water Tower.

The many former workers of the plant who attended my lectures, shared their personal experiences, and provided additional information.

Introduction

The Ford Motor Company operated an assembly plant in Mahwah, NJ from 1955 to 1980. At the time of its completion, it was the largest motor vehicle assembly plant in the United States. The Ford plant along with other early businesses in Mahwah, such as, American Brake Shoe and Foundry Company helped contribute to the economic development of the town and its reputation for low residential property taxes.

Commercial and industrial growth has continued with a constant change in the participants in that arena. Over the years, Mahwah has been the site of many business cycles with new logos and names appearing up and down the main corridors, only to be missing a few years later. During the late 1900's and into the early 2000's corporate growth has steadily continued.

This work is the story of one Mahwah business. Like many others that have come and gone, the Ford Motor Company Assembly Plant, leaves behind memories of a significant period of growth and the changes that have had a lasting effect on the area.

Driving Forces

It was extensive planning of Ford's production and marketing requirements, beginning shortly after World War II, that led to establishment and building of assembly plant in Mahwah, NJ. Ford's economists and market analysts did the initial research which set in motion the company's new expansion programs. They carefully studied all areas in the United States to determine present and future sales trends. Many economic factors were studied in each market, including shifts in population, employment, and income. Over the postwar years, the market researchers saw a rapidly growing demand for automotive products, which meant more business for Ford. With potential new plant construction in mind, the analysts compared labor supplies, railroad, highway, air transportation facilities, water, electric, and fuel resources in all major cities. Manufacturing engineers developed proposed plant projects for these locations and compared costs of operations under several expansion alternatives.

The Ford Executive Committee studied and evaluated the market growth reports and the comparisons of manufacturing resources and costs. Ultimately a pattern of plant locations was selected, which met the current and future requirements of the market, in terms of time, cost, and efficiency. This basic plan provided for the approximate locations of facilities and the output that was needed for each location. It included programs for modernization and expansion of the company's existing facilities in many cities. Where added capacity was needed for a major market, the plan provided for a new plant to be built somewhere within a 100 mile radius of a major distribution center, and it set aside dollars to be spent on each project.[1] In the New York area demand for Ford products had become so great that an entirely new plant was needed. With the New York project authorized by the Executive Committee, several departments of the company tackled the problems of site location and plant design.[2]

---

[1] Ramsey Journal, December 30, 1954, *Ford Tells How Mahwah Site was Selected.*
[2] New York Times, May 6, 1953, *Ford Getting Site for Jersey Plant, pg. 28.*

Site Selection and Design

On May 6, 1953, the Ford Motor Company announced that it planned to build an assembly plant on a 200 acre tract of land in Mahwah, NJ. Ford picked Mahwah for the new 1,960,000 square foot, 1,080 unit per day plant because extensive research convinced Ford's Executive Committee that the site offered the best combination of physical and economic conditions for the project in the New York metropolitan area.[3]

The manufacturing engineering departments, responsible for engineering the manufacturing process needed to meet specific output requirements, planned detailed placement of machines and personnel for maximum efficiency and safety. It determined the flow of materials through processing and assembly stations. Once that phase was completed, Ford called in architects to design a building around the operations, a reversal of the old industry practice of building a factory, and then placing men and machines in it.[4]

The result was a "corn field plant", the name Ford layout engineers had adopted for a newly designed facility planned down to the last detail several months before its site had been selected. Layouts of "Corn field plants" typify the minute detail with which Ford planned a new facility. The layouts stretched across large tables, on which men move back and forth carefully positioning bits of plastic representing, workers, machines, loading docks, supply bins, and other parts forming a detailed scale model of the new plant.[5]

Figure 1 - Architects and designers design the flow through the proposed assembly plant.

---

[3] New York Times, August 12, 1953, *Ford Gets Jersey Site, pg. 41* .
[4] Ramsey Journal, December 30, 1954, *Ford Tells How Mahwah Site was Selected.*
[5] Ibid.

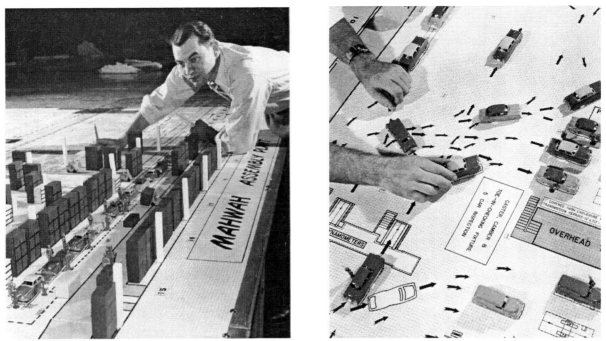

Figure 2 - Architects and designers use scale models to design the proposed assembly plant.

Figure 3 - Architectural artist's rendition of the new Ford assembly plant.

Teams of trained field men visited suggested plant sites within the New York – New Jersey area. They rechecked on the availability of transportation, utilities, and communications for the various proposed sites, as well as, accessibility both to raw materials and the market for finished products. They also investigated such immediate matters as soil conditions to ensure firm foundations and ease of excavations. Findings were turned over to the Executive Committee for a decision on the one best site in the area for the project. The selection of Mahwah cleared the way for purchase of the land, awarding contracts, and actual construction.[6]

The same day that the Ford Motor company announced that Mahwah was selected, the Erie Railroad announced its purchase of the McKee / Ryan property for an estimated $1,000,000. Ford purchased the 177 acre tract of land from the Erie Land and Improvement Company on August 11, 1953. By late August the Erie Railroad was building a rail spur to the plant site with McKee Brothers supplying 250,000 cubic yards of landfill for the tracks.[7]

The Mahwah township committee rezoned the land to make way for the Ford plant. There was little opposition to the rezoning. Some residents expressed concern, but what little opposition there was seemed to be due to the fact that the deal took place quietly and little debate took place prior to rezoning. Anticipating that there may be some opposition, Ford gave the township $320,000 for improvements to the local water systems.

The reasons for the site selection given by the Ford Motor Company were the low tax structure in Mahwah, the availability of labor, water supply, transportation facilities, and adequate space.[8]

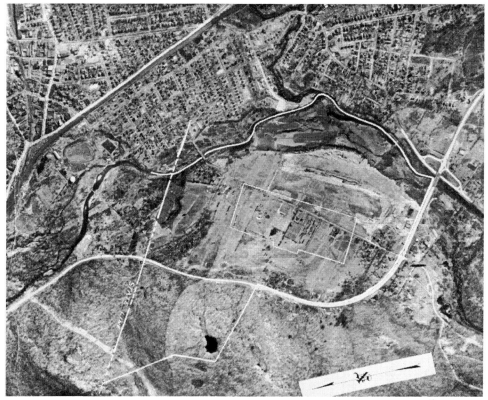

Figure 4 - Aerial view of the selected plant site with the plant outline.[9]

---

[6] Ramsey Journal, December 30, 1954, *Ford Tells How Mahwah Site was Selected.*
[7] Ramsey Journal, August 13, 1953, *Ford Signs Contract With Erie.*
[8] Ramsey Journal, May 6, 1954, *Will the Ford Plant Affect Us.*

Construction

This was a massive two year construction project. I can remember, at a much younger age, spotting the plant out of our family car window on our weekend jaunts from Weehawken, up Route 17, to New York State. I remember being impressed by the enormous scale of the building, as it was being constructed, and in its final form. I often asked my Dad, if Ford was so close by, why did we buy a Pontiac? I don't think I ever got a straight answer. Here's another bit of trivia you may enjoy, on our weekend journey, one of the favored stops was the Red Apple Rest. In those days it was a hub of activity. I remember sitting on the wall out back of the restaurant with an ice cream cone watching the Erie Railroad roll by and counting the cars. Oh well, I guess Game Boys and IPOD's have replaced all of that simple entertainment.

Okay, enough of that, back to the plant construction. The general contract for the construction was awarded to Fred J. Brotherton, Inc., Hackensack, NJ. The contract for structural steel went to Bethlehem Steel, site preparation was awarded to Samuel Braen & Sons, Wyckoff, NJ, and the contract for the boiler house went to Dravo Corp., Pittsburgh, PA. Smaller contracts were awarded to various crafts for smaller elements of the project. Rockland Light and Power Company, Nyack, NY entered into an agreement with Ford to supply electricity to the plant through sub-surface conduits.

The Erie Railroad provided exclusive rail service to the plant. To support this service, the Erie constructed a spur to the plant from the yard at Suffern, NY, over two new bridges, one over the Ramapo River and the other over a private road. The whole length of the spur track was built under contract by Union Building & Construction Company. On the south end of the spur, where extensive sidings were located, the swampy land next to the Ramapo River was filled. Part of the area was filled to a depth of eleven feet to bring the tracks up to the same height as the base grade of the Ford plant.[10]

A new yard at Suffern, named the Hillburn yard, had been built for the plant. The yard consisted of five tracks and was used for classification purposes and had the capacity of 184 cars. The Mahwah yard was adjacent and behind the plant and consisted of seven tracks. It had the capacity for about 280 railroad cars and was used for storage purposes.

The first step was to clear the land and bring in landfill for the building itself and the rail yard that would be built behind the building.

---

[9] Ramsey Journal, December 31, 1953, *Photo – Aerial View of the Proposed Site (Ford Motor Co.)*.
[10] Ramsey Journal, September 3, 1953, *New Erie Spur Track Construction in High Gear*.

Photo – Erie Railroad Magazine, Nov. 1955

Figure 5 - Erie railroad bridge over the Ramapo River between Suffern and Mahwah.

Photo – Tom O'Brien, 2009

Figure 6 - The same bridge as it appears today.

Photo – Erie Railroad Magazine, Nov. 1955

Figure 7 - Erie Railroad bridge over a private road south of Suffern yard.

Photo – Tom O'Brien, 2010

Figure 8 - The same bridge as it appears today.

Photo – Erie Railroad Magazine, Nov. 1955

Figure 9 - The new Erie classification yard at Hillburn

Photo – Erie Railroad Magazine, Nov. 1955

Figure 10 - The new Erie yard in Mahwah adjacent to the Ford plant.

Figure 11 - Clearing the land for construction.

Once the land was cleared and prepared, construction began. The building was constructed like a giant jigsaw puzzle, using pre-formed and pre-cast building sections supported by a steel framework. Bethlehem Steel, having been awarded the contract, started the building process by erecting the steel framework. The structure consisted of 9,500 tons of steel put together with 149,000 high tensile steel bolts.

Figure 12 – The first structural steel sections are placed by Bethlehem Steel[11]

---

[11] Ramsey Journal, February 25, 1954, *Photo – Structural steel erections for the new Ford Plant.*

Next the pre-formed and pre-cast building parts, many of which were fabricated on site, were assembled and added to the steel framework. The building infrastructure, machinery, tanks, pipes, etc. were then installed.

Figure 13 - Pre-formed building parts are lifted into place.

Figure 14 - Giant crane lifts 8 1/2 ton, pre-cast wall section into place.[12]

---

[12] Ramsey Journal, May 20, 1954, *Photo – Crane lifting wall panel into place at Ford plant.*

Figure 15 - Building machinery arrives at the site, ready for installation.

The following scenes were familiar to anyone who lived in the area or drove by on Route 17 during construction.

Figure 16 - Aerial view of the plant nearing completion.

The building process continued for two years. Then, in July of 1955, construction complete, it was time to start operations at the new site.

The Move from the Edgewater Plant

The Ford Motor Company's Edgewater assembly plant, located at 309 River Road, Edgewater, NJ, in southern Bergen County, consisted of a main two story building with more than 1,000,000 square feet of floor area. It also had twenty-five acres of paved outside storage facilities and a railroad siding, it could handle three ocean-going cargo vessels up to 600 feet long, and had a parking area for 1,000 cars.

In 1953, the Ford Company announced to the employees of the Edgewater plant of its plan to build a plant three times larger than the 25 year old plant. A new plant, the announcement said, not only would provide the additional production capacity needed to meet the expanding East coast market for Ford cars and trucks, but also would provide more space and better facilities for employees.[13]

Figure 17 – The Ford assembly plant at Edgewater, NJ.

---

[13] Ramsey Journal, July 14, 1955, *Ford's Move from Edgewater to New Mahwah Plant Starts Today Production to Begin on Tuesday.*

In the months that followed, the plant newsletter carried reports of construction progress at Mahwah and general news about the new location. An information office was set up by the plant's industrial relations department to provide information about the area and housing.

By June 16, 1955, when a survey of the 2,900 Edgewater employees was taken, only 10 employees at Edgewater said that due to early summer retirement they would not take a job at Mahwah. The company and Local 906, United Auto Workers – CIO, completed a transfer agreement under which the union organization from the Edgewater plant would be remain intact and would go along with the new operation.

When Ford moved its assembly operations from Edgewater to Mahwah, NJ over the weekend of July 15, 1955, the employees at the Edgewater plant transferred to the Mahwah plant. Some of the employees had already purchased homes for their families in or near Mahwah, while a majority decided that they already lived close enough to the plant site to make commuting practical. [14]

More than a year of planning went into the huge moving job tackled by the employees of Ford Edgewater plant. The timeline for the move was very specific and well planned:

Edgewater

> Wednesday – July 13
>
> > Approximately 5:00PM – start work of removing and transporting welding jigs.
>
> Thursday – July 14
>
> > Approximately 9:30AM – continue clearing body truck system.
> >
> > Approximately 12:00PM – the paint shop will shut down.
> >
> > Approximately 5:00PM – the trim line will shut down.
>
> Friday – July 15
>
> > Approximately 10:00AM – the final car will roll off the line.
> >
> > Approximately 11:00AM – 25 moving vans leave for Mahwah in truck convoy.

Mahwah

> Saturday and Sunday – July 16 / 17
>
> > New plant receiving and locating equipment.
>
> Monday – July 18
>
> > Continue installation of tools and testing operations.
>
> Tuesday – July 19
>
> > 09:00AM – first official car rolls off the new line at Mahwah.

---

[14] Ramsey Journal, July 14, 1955, *Ford's Move from Edgewater to New Mahwah Plant Starts Today Production to Start Tuesday.*

When it was completed, an overall total of 225 truck and 210 rail carloads of tools, production materials, and office equipment were cleaned, labeled, loaded, hauled, and put in place at the new Mahwah assembly plant. The truck convoys were escorted by police over the route.[15]

Detailed advanced planning made it possible for an employee on the final assembly line to lay down a tool shortly after 3:00PM, Friday, July 15, in Edgewater and pick up that same tool in the new plant 26 miles away on Tuesday morning, July 19, when he/she started work. Coordination of the move extended from the Edgewater plant all the way to the production control organization in Ford's home offices in Dearborn, Michigan. Changeover dates had been fixed all along the line on which Ford's engines, frame, stamping and other manufacturing plants began diverting carloads of parts from Edgewater to Mahwah, so that the Edgewater plant would be left with a minimum stock to transfer to Mahwah on moving day.

At Edgewater, the plant manager, Angus M. Harris, split his management team so it could take on the job of starting the new plant, while it closed the old one. A group of managers was assigned into Mahwah, along with a task force of employees who conducted tests of equipment. Then the group started to load the new conveyors and stock storage areas with production materials as they arrived. The managers who remained behind at Edgewater continued to direct the average daily output of 700 cars and trucks. A special transfer committee defined the final details of the big moving job.

Louis W. Holloway, the Edgewater plant traffic manager, was assigned full time as transfer committee chairman. Other members represented production, engineering, industrial relations, and financial organizations concerned with the move. On March 17, 1955, the committee issued the first of a series of instructions which outlined the moving timetable, and divided the huge task among all departments of the plant.

A major part of the move was handled by the plant's own employees, although some contractors were called to uncouple complicated electrical equipment and reinstall it at Mahwah, or to move out the heaviest machinery and truck it to the new site. An assembly plant actually operates as one big, integrated machine. Each department feeds completed sub-assemblies to the next in the system, until all components come together at the right time at the final assembly line. This meant that at the Edgewater plant, the passenger car body construction department built the last body approximately 26 hours before the body was scheduled to come off the final assembly line as part of the plants last Ford. When the final job was out of the Edgewater welding "bucks", the body building teams immediately began cleaning and packing their tools. Electricians stepped in to disconnect the high voltage welding guns and prepared them for shipment. Then the millwrights placed skids under the 15 ton welding bucks and moved them aboard special heavy duty trailers for the haul to Mahwah. As each successive department down the line finished its

---

[15] Ibid., Ramsey Journal, July 14, 1955

job at Edgewater, the same procedure was followed. By noon Saturday, the transfer committee's timetable called for the last department to be on the road.[16]

Mrs. John A. Walsh (Marie), 58 years old, who had been on the Ford payroll for forty-three years, was behind the wheel of the final car coming off the line at the Edgewater plant. She was accompanied by Edgewater Mayor Milton Lasher and Angus M. Harris, plant manager. A crowd cheered as the gleaming white convertible glided slowly onto the mechanical reception platform. An apprentice whipped a harmonica from his pocket and spiritedly played "The World Turned Upside Down."[17]

Ceiling lights flared to full strength and slowly flickered out. Then the last detail of workers gathered personal belongings and joined in a mass exodus to the new Mahwah assembly plant.[18]

Figure 18 - The last car being assembled at the Edgewater plant.

---

[16] Ramsey Journal, July 14, 1955, *Ford's Move from Edgewater to New Mahwah Plant Starts Today Production to Begin on Tuesday.*
[17] New York Times, July 16, 1955, *Ford Plant Closes at Edgewater with 1,817,938th Car in 25 Years*, pg. 17.
[18] ibid. New York Times, July 16, 1955, pg. 17.

Figure 19 - Milton T. Lasher, Edgewater Mayor; Angus M. Harris, Edgewater/Mahwah Plant Manager; Ms. Marie Walsh drive the last car off the Edgewater line.

Special "operation" offices at Edgewater and Mahwah kept track of the progress for each load. Equipment and tools were marked with tags of various colors indicating the exact area in the new plant in which they were to be placed. In most cases, trucks were loaded with material for only one department, and the vehicles were driven down the wide aisles of the new plant to be unloaded right at the new locations.

The trucks moved over specially mapped routes through Edgewater, Cliffside Park, Fort Lee, and Routes 4 and 17. A Ford supervisor from Edgewater rode with each truck to help get the load through on schedule. Mobile radio cars patrolled the route to call for emergency service, should a breakdown occur.

Day and night throughout the moving operation, cafeterias remained open at both plants to provide hot coffee and meals.

When the Edgewater plant was emptied of tools and stock, small maintenance crews began daubing a protective coating of grease on old machinery, conveyors, and stock racks which were left behind. The process for preparing the 900,000 square foot building at Edgewater for an indefinite period of idleness took several weeks.[19]

---

[19] Ramsey Journal, July 14, 1955, *Ford's Move from Edgewater to New Mahwah Plant Starts Today Production to Begin on Tuesday.*

Figure 20 - The convoy of trucks used during the move from Edgewater to Mahwah.

There were only sixteen hours of production time lost as a result of the move. Cars and trucks were not built for two days, however, there no employees layoffs. Most of them were paid overtime pay for the work they did, related to the move over the weekend.

It cost the Ford Company $150,000 to move from Edgewater to Mahwah, but everything went off on schedule without a hitch, a result of twenty weeks of detailed planning. Eighty percent of equipment, worth over $3,000,000 was transported.

The Edgewater plant was ultimately sold to Irving Maidman, a New York realty investor and K. B. Weisman, a banker, on September 7, 1961. The buyers planned to develop the thirty-three acre property into an industrial and shipping center.

The Mahwah Ford Assembly Plant Goes into Operation

It was July 19, 1955: a time when wherever you looked everything seemed right with America and the world. In midtown Manhattan *The Seven Year Itch* was playing to packed houses at Radio City Music Hall. In Brooklyn, Duke Snyder was about to hit a bottom-of-the-ninth home run into the left-centerfield bleachers of Ebbets Field. And 3,000 miles away in Anaheim, CA, a group of hopeful businessmen were attending to last minute details before opening the doors the next morning on a new enterprise in which all saw great promise: Disneyland. [20]

Meanwhile, in the sleepy New Jersey town of Mahwah, shiny new cars had begun rolling off the newly constructed automobile assembly line all day. The first had presented itself to a crowd of waiting reporters and photographers at 7:57AM. The first car was driven by Mahwah Mayor Charles Feldman, and was followed every 60 seconds, by another and another. At full production the plant would have an average of sixty-vehicles per hour coming off the line. [21]

There was something special about this first car. It was a black station wagon modified for hand driving without any foot operation. It was presented to the Institute of Medical and Physical Rehabilitation of New York University at Bellevue Medical Center for use by paraplegics and other patients with disabilities. One of the first to try it out was a twenty year old patient from Wichita Falls, TX, who was paralyzed from the waist down. Whistling merrily, he swung into the driver's seat and demonstrated how the hand controls made foot movements unnecessary. [22]

Dr. Howard A. Rusk , director of the Institute, explained that the automobile would be used to enable patients to learn to drive with hand controls, "thus providing them means toward a useful and productive life again"[23].

This was the first of what in the following 25 years would become a flood of nearly 6 million cars and trucks to pour from the plant, a factory that seemed at the time to reflect what America was about.

There was a significant impact on the surrounding area. Shortly after the Ford plant opened, small businesses started opening along Route 17. They included gas stations, restaurants, and bars. A related business was also established in Mahwah, the Automobile Conveyance Company, later to become NuCar Carrier Company.

---

[20] Forbes, May 5, 1986, *Mahwah*, John Merwin, pg.68.

[21] ibid.

[22] New York Times, July 19, 1955, *Auto for Crippled Given to Institute.*

[23] ibid.

Figure 21 - Mayor Charles Feldman drives the first car off the line at the new Ford plant.

With the growth of businesses in Mahwah, a small group of business men formed the Mahwah Chamber of Commerce in 1957. This organization still exists today, now known as the Mahwah Regional Chamber of Commerce, with over 500 member companies at the time of this publication.

Dedication and Opening Ceremony

The dedication ceremony of the new automobile and truck assembly plant took place on September 29, 1955. It was a comparatively brief, but impressive ceremony held in front of the new administration building, before a crowd of 14,000 residents, employees, and leaders from New York, New Jersey, and Connecticut.

Figure 22 - Some of the 14,000 attendees at the dedication Ceremony.

Angus M. Harris, plant manager, introduced a bevy of speakers and guests from the dedication platform, which included Henry Ford II, president of the Ford Motor Company; United States Senator Clifford B. Case of New Jersey; Governor Robert B. Meyner; Robert S. McNamara, vice president of the Ford Motor Company; Charles R. Beacham, Ford northeast regional sales manager; Louis D. Crusoe, executive vice president, car and truck division, Ford Motor Company; M. L. Wiesmyer, general manufacturing manager of the company; Frank Garrison, President of the Ford union; and Mayor Charles N. Feldman of Mahwah. An invocation was delivered by Rev. Howard E. Frieby, pastor of the Ramapo Reformed Church.[24]

A group of Erie officials also attended the gala dedication ceremonies. They included H. W. Von Willer, vice president for traffic; M. G. McInnes, vice president for operations and maintenance; A. E. Kriesien, assistant vice president and general manager, Eastern District; E. J. Dean, assistant vice president; D. M. Lynn, assistant vice president; E. C. Hallberg, assistant vice

---

[24] Mahwah Star, September 30, 1955, *14,000 at Ford Dedication; Firm Investing Half-Billion on Expansion.*

president; T. J. Sanok, assistant general manager, Eastern District; B. F. Conway, manager of less-than-carload freight.[25]

Robert S. McNamara, vice president of Ford and general manager of the Ford Division, predicted that the Mahwah plant would be obsolete in 35 years, but in that time it would turn out 8,000,000 cars, worth $18 billion. He said, "The U.S. is on the threshold of the most prosperous era in its history."[26]

Figure 23 - The American flag is raised during the dedication ceremony.

Figure 24 - Governor Robert B. Meyner seated with Henry Ford II and Angus M. Harris, plant manager during the dedication ceremony.

---

[25] Erie Magazine, November, 1955, *Huge Mahwah Ford Plant Opens.*
[26] Mahwah Star, September 30, 1955, *14,000 at Ford Dedication; Firm Investing Half-Billion on Expansion.*

Highlighting the dedication ceremony was the planting of a dogwood tree in memory of Poet Joyce Kilmer, who wrote his famous poem "Trees" while a resident of Mahwah. Participating in the planting of the tree were Robert Kilmer, grandson of the poet; Mahwah Mayor Charles N. Feldman; Henry Ford II, president of the Ford Motor Company; and Ann Kilmer, granddaughter of Kilmer. The tree was dedicated to the growing friendship between community and company.[27]

Figure 25 - Robert Kilmer, grandson of the poet; Mayor Charles N. Feldman; Henry Ford II; and Ann Kilmer, granddaughter of the poet.

Figure 26 – After the dedication ceremony, guests took a tour of the plant.

---

[27] Ramsey Journal, September 30, 1955, *Ford is Staking $500,000,000 in 1956 on Prosperity of U.S.*

Later in the day, Henry Ford II, president of the Ford Motor Company, told 350 New Jersey business and government leaders, at the Swiss Chalet Restaurant in Mahwah, that his firm would spend a half-billion dollars for expansion in 1956 as proof of "our convictions about the future of the American economy". Speaking off the cuff at the dinner given in his honor by the State of New Jersey and the New Jersey State Chamber of Commerce, Mr. Ford said he and his associates at Ford were so confident of the future that they were willing to spend the money to prove it.[28]

Figure 27 - Henry Ford II speaking at the dedication ceremony dinner. Gov. Meyner is seated at the right.

The 1956 expansion dollars would come from earnings and not from borrowings, the company announced. It was believed that the $500,000,000 figure would set a record not only for the company, but for any corporation of Ford's size during any single year.[29]

John C. Williams, president of the State chamber, presided at the four hour long reception and dinner at which Governor Robert B. Meyner shared the spotlight with Mr. Ford.

Commissioner Joseph E. McLean of the New Jersey Department of Conservation and Economic Development told the distinguished gathering that it is not the desire for profits or economic

---

[28] Ramsey Journal, September 30, 1955, *Ford is Staking $500,000,000 in 1956 on Prosperity of U.S.*
[29] ibid.

power that has made the American economy great, but a deep sense of economic responsibility such as Ford has displayed over the years.

Governor Meyner extended the State's official welcome to the automotive firm, while R. L. Healy, chairman of the firm's NY-NJ Community Relations Committee, emphasized that the company attaches a great deal of importance to its community relations and industrial good neighbor programs.

In his talk which concluded the program, Mr. Ford said several times that he felt the company's economic future was unlimited and that he looked for and was counting on an expanding economy, especially in the automobile industry. "Our standard of living has been going up and up, and should continue to do so," he said. "I'm very definitely bullish about the future." Mr. Ford forecast that 1960 would be the year of explosive-like expansion and said that the Mahwah plant was part of his company's expansion program to meet this future market.

In discussing the role of business in this country, Mr. Ford pointed out that the concept of civic responsibility held by American business firms "is almost completely lacking in Europe," where he travelled earlier in the year.[30]

---

[30] Mahwah Star, September 30, 1955, *Confidence in Future Economy of America Cited by Henry Ford.*

The Facility

Ford Division's new Mahwah assembly plant was the third plant in a network of sixteen to be completely engineered with modern materials handling methods to be built in 1955. The plant consisted of a main assembly building, an administration building, an employees' facility building, a power house, and a garage.

Figure 28 - The Main Entrance to the Administration Building. The Kilmer tree is to the right.

Figure 29 - The Main Entrance and Administration Building

The plant was built on a 177 acre tract of land. The Main assembly building covered 40 acres of land and had more than 1,960,000 square feet of manufacturing space.[31]

---

[31] Ramsey Journal, July 21, 1955, *Mahwah Ford Plant Covers 177 Acres.*

For cleanliness and quiet, the plant's employee service facilities were located in a special building section between the manufacturing section and the administration building. There were three cafeterias capable of accommodating more than 2,000 persons at once, one of which stayed open 24 hours a day. The employees consumed 450 pounds of meat, 330 pounds of vegetables, 100 gallons of soup, 350 gallons of coffee, 26 loaves of bread, 650 rolls, and 165 pies every workday.[32]

A plant hospital was located just off the manufacturing floor. It contained all the equipment needed to treat employees who were injured or became ill on the job. The medical facility was staffed with a physician, three nurses, two first aiders, and a secretary to maintain records. When the production schedule required, the hospital was open 24 hours. There was in-plant ambulance on standby to move to the scene of a plant accident or to transport employees to other medical facilities when needed.

Four large locker rooms contained more than 5,000 individual lockers for employees. Subways under the final assembly line allowed employees to walk directly from central areas of the building to the employee service area, without having to skirt the ends of the long final assembly line.

In a building as large as the assembly plant, distances were so great that special transportation was provided for supervisors and work crews who had to cover the wide area. Six electric three wheel cars kept the managers mobile. Messengers rode bicycles, and maintenance and emergency crews had gas powered scooters so they could respond to situations quickly throughout the plant.

Figure 30 - View down the line.

---

[32] The Evening News, 1962, *Ford Mahwah Plant, a City that Never Sleeps.*

At the rear of the plant, the power house, tall as a three story building, had three automatic oil fired boilers to supply steam for production equipment, cafeterias, and sanitary uses. More than 34,500 gallons of oil were consumed during a working day, particularly during the winter months. The boilers had standby burners for conversion to gas if the oil supply was interrupted. Separate gas-fired units within the plant were used for space heating, enamel drying ovens, and spray booths, consuming more than 1,200,000cubic feet of gas each working day.. Every production day the plant consumed 235,320 kilowatt hours of electricity. At that time, it was enough to satisfy the electrical requirements of the city the size of Passaic. The plant and offices were illuminated by 37,328 fluorescent tubes and 704 light bulbs that needed constant monitoring and replacement. Maintaining all this power were more than 50 electricians who needed to be familiar with every circuit, outlet, button, and switch along the 757 miles of wiring.[33]

Smaller buildings provided storage space outside the plant for oxygen, acetylene, oil, paint, and gasoline. The fluids and gases were pumped into the plant through 18 pipelines feeding various departments.

Passenger car and truck assembly systems were completely separate, each including such auxiliary operations as wheel painting, tire mounting, engine dress-up, cushion assembly, and front end sub-assembly. Separation of the two systems was adopted by Ford manufacturing engineers for a number of economy reasons, among them being advantages in stock distribution, line job mixing, adaptability to automatic material handling systems, and supervision.

The passenger car production system occupied more than 1,030,000 square feet of floor space and was spread over three-fifths of the assembly building. The system was capable of producing 1080 units per day on a two-shift, 16 hour basis, when to market demand required the volume.

It contained approximately 11 miles of conveyor systems. Conveyor lengths and speeds throughout the plant were based on research done long before the plant was built.

Assignment of stock areas and width of aisles was done as part of a carefully developed materials handling plan, which took into consideration the requirements at each work location on the production lines, as well as, reserve stock space, transporting and handling. Almost two-thirds of the plant's manufacturing space was devoted to these aisles and stock storage areas. The system provided an eight hour supply of stock for each assembly line operator. The plant had ten miles of aisles space.

Specific advancements in materials handling included the use of automatic conveyor transfers throughout the plant, automatic paint spraying of small parts, and automatic tire mounting.

---

[33] The Evening News, 1962, *Ford Mahwah Plant, a City that Never Sleeps.*

The plant was designed to receive more than 9,000 individual parts and sub-assemblies that went into the various cars and trucks made there. At full capacity, that amounted to 4,500 tons of material a day. Most of the plant's production materials arrived by rail in a dock area 2,117 feet long by 90 feet wide. Two depressed tracks ran the entire length of the east side of the building, with docks on each side. Five ton traveling cranes were installed over the tracks at each end of the building. Between these two cranes on the receiving dock were several smaller bridge cranes. Five hydraulic lift bridges 15 feet wide could be used to cross the railroad depression.

The order in which the railcars entered the plant was critically important. A large railroad car storage and sorting yard was built behind the plant that could handle about 280 cars. Positioning on the train and the sequence the rail cars would enter the building was handled in this yard.

Car loads of engines and frames must be placed in the train so that they stopped opposite the engine department and frame assembly line at the south end of the building. Cars of body stampings had to be facing the body construction department in the center of the plant. Truck engines and body parts had to be in the cars stopping at the north end of the building.

A truck dock, capable of handling 18 trucks at once, was also on the east side of the building. Each truck spot was equipped with a 20,000 pound capacity hydraulic dock leveler which could be raised or lowered to match the truck bed height.[34]

In older automotive plants, parts were moved from rail docks to assembly locations by means of overhead conveyors. These fixed installations required a lot of maintenance. If the plant had to be rearranged to meet a production change, moving them was time consuming and expensive.

In the Mahwah plant, the conveyors were replaced by tow-trains drawn by small tractors through the broad aisles leading to the production and stock areas.

Once the motorized tow trains left the rail dock, they ran on regular routes through the plant. At the engine department, high lift trucks would pick steel racks, each bearing four car engines, off the tow trains and stack them as high as eighteen feet in the air, until they were needed on the production line. Racks of body side panels, stacked on end when they were unloaded from the rail cars, were parked on their wheeled carriers in reserve areas near the body welding jigs.

New material handling equipment made it easier to supply the more complex needs of the modern assembly line, but it was still the conveyor which made mass production possible. It carried engines, bodies, frames, wheels, and finally the complete chassis past employees who added part after part until the car was finished.

---

[34] Erie Magazine, November, 1955, *Huge Mahwah Ford Plant Opens*, Pgs. 4,10, and 11

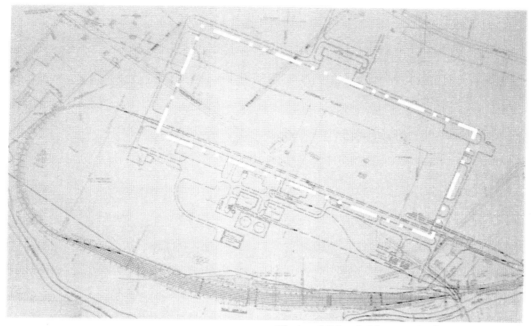

Photo – Mahwah Museum Society / Robert Adler
Figure 31 - Diagram of the railroad system. (Plant boundaries outlined).

Photo – Robert Adler
Figure 32 - View of the rail yard behind the Ford plant. Freight cars to be sorted are in the background. The plants water tower is visible on the right.

Where men once tugged at heavy car bodies to move them from one conveyor line to another, automatic transfer devices in the newer plants, including Mahwah, shunted the bodies between long chain link systems to be rust proofed, prime painted, finish painted, two toned, and equipped with interior fabric and chrome trim.[35]

---

[35] Ramsey Journal, July 28, 1955, *New Mahwah Ford plant is a Miracle of Modern Planning and Design.*

Operations

General Production Schedule

When the plant first opened, it operated with a single shift of operators, usually on extended schedules or overtime. When the plant reached full production at the beginning of 1956, the plant went on a two shift operation, allowing almost all of the original and new employees to work a regular eight hour shift.

Fluctuations in market demand directly affected the operations at the plant. It was fairly common for the Ford management to cancel a shift, a whole day, or longer of production and lay off hundreds and sometimes thousands of workers when the car market demand fell. Truck assembly and plant maintenance personnel experienced fewer lay-offs.

Model Changeover

During the summer months, usually in August for the Ford plant in Mahwah, production stopped and the assembly lines were extensively changed in preparation for the new model year vehicles.

The parking lots were virtually empty. There were no cars in the storage yards awaiting delivery. Inside the plant, huge parts storage areas were empty and the assembly line rested quietly. But the calm was on the surface only. There were pockets of activity throughout the plant because here were the beginnings of furious preparations for production of the first cars of the next model year.

Huge excavations pockmarked the floor where new machines would appear and assembly line improvements would be made. The first of the new metal body parts arrive and production engineers clustered intently around the first assembled bodies, poring over intricate blueprints as they acquainted themselves with the first new cars they would build for public introduction the coming fall. Many of these people along with key hourly employees, had already taken one to four weeks of intensive familiarization courses, in Dearborn, MI, to prepare for the job of training each assembly line worker for his/her new tasks.

It is during this time that most of the employees took their summer vacations, some were laid off. The steel industry and many other downstream suppliers slowed or shut down while the automobile plants closed to retool for the model changeover.[36]

---

[36] Home and Store News, August 21, 1968, *Ford Plant is in Changeover.*

On the Line

A tour through an assembly plant is a backstage experience. Going through the Ford plant at Mahwah, visitors were overwhelmed and felt a sense of being small by the magnitude of everything around them: thousands of motors, ceiling high stacks of transmissions, acres of tires, layers of metal, all moving into place on the assembly line in a deafening roar. Overhead giant tracks, cranes, and other gear easily swung motors, frames and chassis into position.

Freight trains with parts from a variety of suppliers rolled in at the rate of eighty-four cars a day with a regularity reminiscent of the arrival and departure schedules maintained at major terminals. These deliveries were supplemented by huge trailer-trucks and other delivery vehicles that pulled up to eighteen loading ramps at the rear and side entrances of the assembly plant.

Inside the plant, pedestrian traffic hopped aboard a variety of small transports, including tricycles, motor carts, and fork lift trucks. There were 173 pieces of motorized transports, plus pedal cycles.

But for all the automation that marked assembly line production, the worker continued to be the key element. The worker not only pushed the buttons that motivated the cable hooks needed to lift one part on to another, but also spot welded body parts with compressed air guns that hung overhead like chandeliers. The attention to detail to this phase of the assembly was emphasized, for example, in the welding of the roof. Each roof was given 300 spot welds to make it part of the frame of the car. Similar hand welding was done around other sections of the body where stress called for extra spot welding to strengthen the over-all body structure.

Skilled and semi-skilled workers were among the crews and teams that fit glass into frames, wired up panels, finished metal trims, soldered body joints, and touched up the mirror finish body paint as the cars came through the fray of assembly.

Many of these workers were skilled in more ways than one. A former employee related a story to me about one of the fellows who worked near the enamel drying ovens, who considered himself quite the gourmet chef. Once a week he would bring in steaks wrapped in foil, placed them in the ovens with the auto body parts for just the right amount of time, producing perfectly cooked, juicy, steaks for he and some of his co-workers. People always knew when the special steak day was because you could smell the steaks cooking in that area of the plant. This was a fellow everyone wanted to become friends with.

Job assignment changes were frequent, sometimes done to prevent boredom, other times to allow for more income, perhaps five cents an hour for a minor change in task. Promotions occurred at times for unexpected reasons. One such incident happened when a line worker was having a discussion with the team leader about how a particular task could be simplified that would save time and money, without compromising quality. The team leader wasn't buying it. Unknown to both, a line manager was standing nearby listening to the discussion. He pulled the worker off to the side and asked if he had any other ideas, which he did. Shortly after the discussion, the worker was promoted to Foreman.

At the end of the line, when the car was ready for delivery to the dealer, laboratory workers ran the vehicles through the paces, testing and checking every part, Their results were recorded on a "Final Acceptance Inspection Card" that contained twenty-one interior check items, eleven exterior items, twelve rear of the vehicle items, and thirteen front items.

Inspectors raced the engines, jammed on the brakes, fidgeted with the seat springs and dashboard switches that controlled the lights, radio, and if the car had it, the air-conditioning installation. If the mirror-gloss finish of the car body had a suggestion of a scratch, if the brakes pulled off center just a fraction, if the dashboard wiring was loose, if the weather stripping was wrinkled – back went the car to the particular section where the wrong could be righted.

Even if there was nothing wrong with the cars that flowed off the line, inspectors would pull a car off the line every now and then and tear it apart. They would cut off the roof with acetylene torches and count the spot welding marks, remove the doors to check the tightness and number of screws, and in general check on virtually every assembly operation.

Conditions on the Line

The environment was hot and noisy. One prior Ford employee said that the plant was not air conditioned, therefore, particularly during the summer months, it was extremely hot. Workers at time wore only a tee shirt and shorts, and still perspired a lot. There were fans throughout the plant, but they just couldn't do the job.

On September 5, 1961, more that 2,000 assembly workers at the plant walked out after lunch, forcing a halt to operations. The men started reporting to the medical department at lunch time, complaining about the heat, which climbed to a high of 94 degrees. Shortly after the lunch hour, men began leaving the plant. The commercial and passenger vehicle lines were forced to shut down. Union leaders declined to comment on the walkout, but both company and union officials said it had nothing to do with contract negotiations between the United Auto workers and Ford in Detroit. The night crew reported to work on schedule.

The noise was another uncomfortable factor. Depending on your location in the plant and the machinery you were working near, the noise could be deafening. Sometime it was difficult to talk to someone right next to you without yelling.

Figure 33 - Workers functioned above and below the cars as they rolled down the line. Parts supply bins were nearby.

Figure 34 - Each worker on the line had a specific task to perform on the car as it rolled by.

Figure 35 - A 1974 Ford LTD nears the end of the line.

Figure 36 - A final test and inspection is done on each car before it leaves the plant.

The pace was always fast. The people on the line had a particular job to do on the passing cars or trucks and the movement of the vehicles was constant. Any distraction could cause a break in the flow and the pace would quicken so that the individual job was completed before the vehicle moved on. At times it seemed that the line moved faster. The push for production was always a priority.

Safety

Within the first four years of operation, Safety Engineers at the assembly plant equipped employees with some 116 separate categories of safety equipment to promote good health and safety practices. The challenge for the Safety Engineers was to surround each occupation with every known safeguard and then educate the workers to think and act safely, both on the job and in their off the job pursuits.

Their stock in trade included such items as individually fitted ear plugs, lead grinders' hoods, and special shoes. Tool repair men were kept busy repairing safety goggles and masks or taking the necessary stitch in time to keep an item of safety equipment serviceable and available when needed.

Goggles and safety glasses of every description were evident throughout the plant. For example, welder goggles were worn under welders' hoods. Other types included acid free type rubber frame goggles fitted with nose guards for use around acids, caustics, and irritating fumes.

Chip welders wore case hardened safety glasses under their welders' goggles to prevent intrusion of flying chips of steel into their eyes. All of the eight varieties of safety glasses conformed to optical standards laid down by the optical industry. The list of other equipment available was long and included everything from hand creams to foul weather gear.

Training supervisors gave mandatory courses in safe working practices to new foreman and refresher courses to veteran foreman to pass along to their employees. For the safety engineers, the rewards came when they got home each night and thought of the "might have been" accidents that were prevented by their constant vigilance. Safety improvements and new innovations were routine at the plant.[37]

As part of the overall safety standards instituted at the plant, departmental fire fighting brigades were organized to go into action if fire should break out in the plant. Training of these brigades was an important part of the fire safety program which had been in operation since the plant opened. The plant was equipped with more than 1,100 portable extinguishers. These included water and dry chemical powder, in addition to carbon dioxide extinguishers. There were also about 108 hose reels for protection of the plants manufacturing area. Augmenting this fire protection equipment were one hose and chemical truck, one in-plant, fire truck, seven 150-pound dry chemical wheeled extinguishers, and eight hose carts containing 250 feet of 2 ½ inch hose.[38]

Fully trained and organized to move in and use this equipment in case of a fire were two plant brigades for the day shift and two brigades for the night shift. This was the first implementation of brigades. More were added later to cover all hazardous storage and manufacturing areas in the plant. All members of these brigades were volunteers and were trained to handle any fire emergency. Inspection and maintenance of the fire-fighting equipment at the plant was a full time job for the men who make up the fire protection section. At the time, 1955, James Kolchin was fire inspection officer for the day shift and Joseph Kaufman was the fire chief for the night shift. They were assisted by two members of the maintenance department, Richard Craig and Leon Lefebvre. In addition to formulating the brigade program, conducting regular drills, and constantly checking the equipment, the fire protection section was concerned with daily inspection of all areas and buildings at the plant.

---

[37] Ramsey Journal, July 9, 1959, *Safety Assured at Ford Plant by Work of 2 Men Using Many Different Kinds of Equipment*.

[38] Ridgewood Herald News, August 2, 1956, *Ford Organizes Fire Brigades in Plant*

In February, 1956 the Ford Motor company received the award of honor for its outstanding safety record from the National Safety Council for operating its Edgewater-Mahwah plants for 4,563,561 man hours without a disabling accident. Carl Holderman, Commissioner of the New Jersey Department of Labor and Industry, presented the award to Angus M. Harris, plant manager, and Edward L. Jones, safety engineer, in ceremonies at the Mahwah plant. This was the first of many varied awards given for safety at the plant.

Milestones and Significant Events

1950's

July 19, 1955 – 7:57AM – The first car rolls off the assembly line at the Mahwah plant.

The plant was now in operation, employing a single day shift. Plans were in place to add a second night shift when the plant reached full production.[39]

January 3, 1956 – A second shift is started.

The new plants at Mahwah and Louisville added a second shift and started sixteen hour days of operation, adding about 2,500 employees. This also provided an opportunity to promote about 170 employees to supervisory positions. At the same time, employees returned to a regular eight hour day. Most had been working on an overtime basis for more than a year.[40] [41]

August 8, 1956 – The 200,000th Ford is produced at the Mahwah Ford plant.

A shiny new white Ford Fairlane convertible rolled off the line at the Mahwah plant as the 200,000th car produced at the facility since its opening. As it was driven off the line, Patricia Elmira Campbell, Miss New Jersey 1955, rode as a passenger.

Figure 37 - The 200,000th car rolls off the line at Mahwah.

---

[39] New York Times, July 17, 1955, *First Ford Rolls in Mahwah Plant.*

[40] New York Times, October 6, 1955, *Ford Plant to add Shift*

[41] New York Times, December 23, 1955, *Ford Adding 2D Shift*

July 15, 1957 – The first Edsel rolls off the line at Mahwah.

Back in 1956, Ford Motor Company realized that there was a void in their selections of mid-size automobiles. While Chevrolet owners could "move up" to a Buick, Pontiac or Oldsmobile, and Dodge owners could advance to a Plymouth or Chrysler, Ford buyers were looking at the Mercury alone. The perception was that Ford was losing customers to other manufacturers when the time came to trade-up. In order to correct the problem, Ford instituted plans for an entirely new car division, and an entirely new car. The design was to be completely unique, distinguishable from any angle. And the promotional build-up of the car would be like nothing else.

The 1958 Edsel came in two sizes – big and bigger! The Senior Series cars were the Citation and Corsair models. They were built on the large Mercury-based frame. The Junior Series cars were Rangers, Pacers, and station wagons Bermuda, Villager, and Roundup, which were built on the smaller Ford-based frame. One of the most talked about features was the Teletouch shifter, which controller the automatic transmission selection electronically from push buttons in the center of the steering wheel hub. A series of planetary gears in the column kept the buttons stationary as the wheel turned. Many other Edsel-original ideas are still found on today's cars. The car was referred to as the "E" car, for Experimental, from its inception. The name "Edsel" was bestowed by Special Products Division General Manager Richard Krafve, after reviewing a list of nearly 8,000 suggestions from their advertising firm, Ford employees and renowned poet Marianne Moore who was solicited for ideas. The car was named after Henry Ford's son, Edsel Bryant Ford. 110,847 Edsels were built before the company pulled the plug after three years due to lack of sales and negative press. Ironically, market research conducted just a few years earlier had pointed to the Edsel's success; consumers had said they wanted more horsepower, tailfins, three-tone paint jobs, and wraparound windshields. However, by 1957, fickle consumers had changed their minds, and despite a relatively low price, Edsel sales lagged.

Figure 38 - The first seven Edsels were assembled in Mahwah.

- o Floating speedometer that glows when a pre-set speed limit is exceeded
- o Transmission locks in park until ignition key turned (new with Edsel - still used today)
- o Top portion of seats slant forward to provide shoulder support
- o Triple-thermostat cooling system (head/block/radiator) during warm-up for increased fuel economy & heater performance (E-475 engine)
- o Front-mounted distributor, coil, fuel pump, oil filter dipstick for easy access
- o Hood hinged in the front for safety (Although this somewhat limits access to the aforementioned distributor, etc!)
- o Hood release controlled electronically, from inside the car
- o The front seats were split 60/40 for better driver comfort
- o Promoted Self-Adjusting brakes as a safe and convenient method of compensating for normal brake lining wear. This mechanism has been used in drum brake systems ever since. (They were not, however, an Edsel invention as is commonly thought. The same basic design was introduced on the 1948 Studebaker.)
- o A HUGE array of bells and whistles available as options

Photo – Tom O'Brien
Figure 39 - An Edsel like the first one built.

Seven pilot cars were produced in May 1957. Surviving Mahwah Edsels are **quite** rare, mainly because they were sold on the eastern seaboard and were victims of salt and harsh winters.

In a pre-planned corporate publicity promotion, the first Edsel was sold at 12:01AM, September 4, 1957, to a Dr. and Mrs. Frank Zeller of Winter Haven, FL, who were good friends of the Ford family. Unfortunately, as the turquoise and white Pacer convertible drove off into the darkness of the early morning, it promptly ran out of gas as the dealer had forgotten to fill the gas tank in all the mass confusion of the previous day.

April 7, 1958 – Fire at the plant.

On April 7, 1958, a fire broke out in the foam rubber storage area. Firemen ran hoses over the roof to get at the blaze as smoke poured out of vents in the roof. Both Mahwah and Ramsey Fire Departments responded to the alarm and were able to contain the blaze to a small section of the plant. The fire shut down production. All employees except the executives and clerical help were sent home. The plant reopened day and night operations the next morning. Rumors indicated that the fire may have been deliberately set. Tires stuffed with gasoline soaked rags were supposedly found in the area.

Figure 40 - Fire breaks out in the foam rubber storage area.[42]

October 23, 1958 – Model "T" built at the Mahwah plant.

Assembly workers put together a Model T of the 1909 vintage, painted red, to celebrate the 50th Anniversary of the world's best selling automobile model. About 15,000,000 were produced between October, 1908 and 1927, when the Model A supplanted it.[43]

---

[42] Ramsey Journal, April 10, 1958, *Photo – Fire at the Ford Motor Company Assembly Plant in Mahwah*

[43] New York Times, October 24, 1958, *Jersey Ford Plant Reassembles One of 15,000,000*, Bernard Stengren.

The reassembly involved finding the body and chassis in Flint, MI, and buying them from John Skaff, a furniture dealer and antique car hobbyist. A coast to coast search of antique shops uncovered such items as the brass lamps needed to fit the car out properly. But the leather work, including the seats and convertible top, and four wooden wheels had to be replaced by custom shops. While the ancient "T" was on the 720 auto-a-day assembly line, the contrasts with modern models were sharp, in many respects. The reassembly was done by six mechanic supervisors, and the parts were handled with tender, loving care, instead of by overhead hoists and conveyors.

Figure 41 - 50th Anniversary Model "T" was built at the Ford plant in Mahwah.

During the celebration, a parade of vintage Ford cars was held. Driving the lead car was Irving Nelson, the oldest employee at the plant at 63. Mr. Nelson assembled Model T's forty years prior and drove one until 1925.

The newly assembled Model T was taken to Dearborn, MI, for permanent display at the Henry Ford Museum of the Edison Institute.

Figure 42 - Irving Nelson ready to start the parade.

Figure 43 - Irving Nelson gives some instruction on starting the Model "T" to Samuel Simmons, plant manager.

Figure 44 - Ready to roll.

Figure 45 - The parade of vintage cars.

Figure 46 - Taking a spin down the old Route 17.

1960's

During the ten years following the plants opening, its approximately 5,100 employees had earned nearly one-third of a billion dollars. Total annual payroll in 1964 was $35,772,361. Plant manager, Owen T. Blunt, stated that the site had become one of the most productive and economically dynamic operations in modern industrial history. He referred to it as "a stadium of industrial skills".

However, the plant was not without its problems. In 1960, six factory workers were arrested and accused of taking over $100,000 worth of auto parts over the last two years. The six were arrested by the Federal Bureau of Investigation. David Klingsberg, assistant United States attorney, said the men had smuggled small parts such as voltage regulators, high-tension coils and directional signal lights out of the plant by concealing them under their jackets. He said that the articles had been stored in their homes until sold in large lots to dealers in New York. About $30,000 worth of the articles were recovered. Supervisors of the plant expressed amazement that so much in small parts could be sneaked past the security guards.[44]

The 1,000,000th car assembled at the Mahwah plant is driven off the line.

In 1960, five years after the plant opening, the 1,000,000th car assembled at the Mahwah plant, a shiny new white Fairlane convertible, was driven off the line.

---

[44] New York Times, January 31, 1960, *6 Held in Looting at Ford Factory.*

Figure 47 - The 1,000,000th car is driven off the line.

The Ford plant had averaged a daily dollar amount of 43 million and an annual dollar volume of $700 million. During the celebration of the 10th Anniversary celebrations and despite all the notable statistics, the mood was "business as usual" as it prepared for the production of its 1966 models. The plant produced its last 1965 car and truck on Friday, July 25, 1965, and with a special staff of technicians and maintenance personnel, started immediately to begin preparations to launch its first 1966 car on Monday, August 16, 1965.

At the time, Ford's largest plant supplied Ford dealers from the northern tip of Maine in New England to the District of Columbia with a complete line of Ford Galaxie passenger cars, as well as, special orders for police cars and taxis. In addition, it produced light and medium trucks for distribution and sales over much of the eastern seaboard. The plant also prepared and crated vehicles for shipment to overseas dealers.

At the beginning of 1967, lagging automobile sales prompted adjusting production levels to less than full production. Layoffs and shortened work weeks were commonplace in the auto industry.

March 9 1960 – Ford gets Army contract.

The ordinance Tank Command awarded a $2,402,013 to the Ford Motor Company for 1,065 pickup trucks. Part of the work was done at the Ford Mahwah assembly plant.[45]

September 8, 1961 – Ford sells the Edgewater plant.

The Edgewater plant was ultimately sold to Irving Maidman, a New York realty investor and K. B. Weisman, a banker, on September 7, 1961. The buyers planned to develop the thirty-three acre property into an industrial and shipping center.[46]

---

[45] New York Times, March 9, 1960, *Ford Gets Army Work*.

April 14, 1963 – Ford shares in two Armed Forces truck contracts.

The Ford Motor Company Mahwah assembly plant shares in two Armed forces truck contracts for pickup trucks. The Mahwah plant would produce a total of 405 trucks.[47]

July, 1965 – 10th Anniversary of the Mahwah plant opening.

During the ten years since its opening, the Mahwah plant assembled 2,211,551 cars and trucks, 393,613 more than the old Edgewater plant it replaced had produced in 25 years. The milestone car, a Galaxie 500, white convertible was driven off the line by plant manager, Owen T. Blunt.[48]

Figure 48 - Owen T. Blunt, plant manager, drives the 10th Anniversary car off the line.

August 9, 1968 – Truck recall.

On August 9, 1968, the Ford Motor Company issued a recall of 14,600 pickup trucks to correct a possible safety defect. The 1968 trucks of the F-250 and F-350 Series were built at Ford's Mahwah and Kansas City plants. Those plants used the wrong types of nuts in attaching the pickup box to the frame. The defect was discovered after a report that one camper unit, which was places atop the pickup, fell off.[49]

---

[46] New York Times, September 8, 1961, *Plant in New Jersey is Sold by Ford,* pg. 51
[47] New York Times, April 15, 1963, *Ford Shares in Contract,* pg. 57.
[48] The Journal, July 16, 1965, *Ford Plant Celebrates 10th Year,* pg. 6.
[49] New York Times, August 10, 1968, *Ford Recalls 14,600 Trucks for Possible Safety Defect,* pg. 10.

1970's

Early 1970's – Mahwah loses Taxi Cab contract.

In the early '70's the fleet of vehicles that the assembly men built also included New York City taxi cabs. Because of poor workmanship in the Ford plant in Mahwah, production of the cabs switched to Norfolk, VA, because of their reputation for high quality workmanship.

August 11, 1977 – Plant tours resume after ten years.

Governor Brendan T. Byrne helped inaugurate the first public tour program at Ford Motor Company's assembly plant in more than ten years. On August 11, 1977, the governor rode in the lead car of a four car tour train which carried plant officials and Mahwah Cub Scouts through Granada, Monarch and light truck assembly lines.

Guided tours of the plant were taken on a 36-passenger tour train equipped with speakers in each row of the seats, and a running commentary described the production operations. The tours proceeded through twelve miles of assembly conveyor lines filled with engines, car bodies, and many other automotive parts, and were approximately one hour in duration.

Visitors observed such assembly operations as vinyl roof installation and body trimming; an automatic welding complex, in which the underbody car structure received 400 welds in under one minute; engine decking, the installation of a thousand pound engine and transmission unit in a single procedure; and body decking, the overhead transfer of car bodies onto the final assembly line where they were installed on rear axles. At the end of the line, visitors viewed Granadas and Monarchs driven off for testing and inspection at the rate of one a minute.[50] [51]

June 25, 1978 – Ford holds gala to honor its workers at Mahwah.

A celebration commemorating Ford Motor Company's 75th Anniversary, held at the Mahwah assembly plant drew a crowd of 7,100 Ford employees and their families. Among the attractions at the family day event were 40 antique cars as well as current car and truck models. Tours of the plant were offered, along with refreshments, live music, and free gifts for children. There were also showings of "The World of Ford," a film marking the company's 75th year of operations. Employees displayed products of their hobbies, including paintings, photographs, needlepoint, and various collections. A spokesman for the company stated, "We decided to celebrate with all the employees. They're obviously the ones who make us successful."[52]

---

[50] Home and Store News, August 24, 1977, *Ford Plant Open for Tours.*

[51] Home and Store News, November 11, 1977, *Mahwah Ford has Plant Tours.*

[52] The Reporter, June 29, 1978, *Ford Gala Honors Workers.*

1980's

May 5, 1980 – Senator Edward Kennedy speaks at rally at Mahwah Ford Plant.

Senator Edward M. Kennedy stood before the sprawling Ford Motor Company assembly plant in Mahwah, which was scheduled to close the following month, and called it "the clearest example of the bankrupt, failed and flawed economic policies of Jimmy Carter." He said that the fiscal policies of the Carter Administration had made it difficult for prospective automobile buyers to finance a purchase and for dealers to stock their showrooms.[53]

Senator Kennedy met with leaders of several union locals in New Jersey and several public officials before addressing a mid-afternoon rally of the United Automobile Workers Union at the plant. The rally, scheduled at the time of a shift change, attracted more than 2,000 assembly line workers. A Democrat of Massachusetts, Kennedy said his appearances in New Jersey on that day were the start of his campaign for the June 3rd Presidential primary in the state.

Figure 49 - Senator Edward M. Kennedy addressing employees at the Mahwah Ford plant.

---

[53] New York Times, May 5, 1980, *Kennedy Says Carter Fiscal Policy Doomed Auto Plant in New Jersey*

There should have been excitement in the air when Kennedy spoke. However, for the most part, the workers who were coming in for the night shift or those leaving for the day, simply stood and watched. The audience was polite and responded with cheers on a few occasions, but the overall impression left by the exercise was one of helplessness.[54]

Kennedy called the automobile industry "the backbone of American industrial strength" and recalled that workers at the Mahwah plant had been on an overtime schedule the previous summer. Since January, 1980, 1,200 workers who assembled light trucks had been laid off. They were to be joined by the remaining 3,700 plant workers in June, 1980.

"The figures here are typical of the 250,000 automobile workers who lost their jobs as of today and the 50,000 more who will be out of work by next month and the 50,000 additional by the beginning of the following month," Senator Kennedy remarked.

Figure 50 - Senator Edward M. Kennedy.

June 20, 1980, The Ford Motor Company Mahwah assembly plant closes .[55]

After 25 years, on June 20, 1980, the Ford Motor Company's plant at Mahwah, NJ closed.

The bad news broke at midday, April 17, 1980. Several hundred professional and administrative employees at the plant, trooped quietly into the spacious auditorium that workers called the

---

[54] New York Times, May 11, 1980, *Exercise in Futility*, Joseph Sullivan, pg. NJ11.
[55] New York Times, June 21, 1980, *Last Ford Leaves Mahwah Plant; 4,500 Employees Lose Their Jobs.*,pg. 1, 26.

theatre, sat down, and heard a grim faced plant manager, A. J. Caprara, tell them they had just lost their jobs. "I want to thank each of you for your past contributions and solicit your cooperation during the shutdown process," he concluded, reading from a company statement that was distributed to 3,700 workers.

The day shift heard the announcement at 2:30 p.m. The night shift was greeted with the news at 3:45 p.m., when the men and women reported for work, though it was hardly news by then.

Inside the plant, work went on as usual, as Ford cars were assembled in what was described as a subdued atmosphere. Outside, in a windy parking lot awash in cars, the workers commiserated with one another about the crush of coming mortgage payments, college tuition bills, and alimony payments – all the little everyday obligations that suddenly took on a new significance.

The Union and Job Actions

The UAW signed its first contract with Ford Motor Company in 1941 after years of confrontation between labor and management. The first director of the UAW Ford Department was Richard Leonard, a welder from Ohio who had been active in organizing automobile industry workers since the 1930s. A casualty of UAW factionalism, Leonard lost his position to Highland Park Local 400 president Ken Bannon in 1947, who remained director until his retirement in 1980. The UAW Ford Department achieved many gains for Ford employees, including a pension plan, health care benefits, workplace health and safety protection, skilled trade recognition, a shortened work week, more paid days off, supplemental unemployment benefits, and a guaranteed annual income credit. The union organization at the assembly plant was local 906 of the United Automobile Workers. A new employee to the plant had to work there for three months before he/she was eligible to join the Union.

Not unlike any other unionized business, strikes and other labor actions, large and small, took place with an almost predictable frequency. Below are listed several of the actions taken at the Ford plant in Mahwah.

Strike vote taken in favor of walkout – December 10, 1957.

A strike at the Ford Motor Company plant in Mahwah was voted by the members of the United Auto Workers. Involved were twenty-one health and safety grievances, wages and rates for work on retractable convertibles and twenty-one work standard grievances. The results were 4 to 1 in favor of the strike, according to Thomas F. Bladen, local president.[56]

Figure 51 - Strikers stop to talk to a plant employee in his new 1957 Ford.

---

[56] New York Times, December 11, 1957, *Ford Strike is Voted.*

Figure 52 - A few words are exchanged with the owner of a GM car.

Figure 53 - The pickets walk away from another GM vehicle owner in his Pontiac.

Ford Strike Averted – November 19, 1960.

A scheduled strike at the Mahwah Ford assembly plant was averted when members of Local 906, United Auto Workers, voted in support of an agreement reached by union negotiators and management. The ratification came at a meeting at the Schuetzen Casino in North Bergen, and concluded twelve days of negotiations.[57]

Eighty- eight plants and facilities go on strike – October 3, 1961.

Ford announced that its operations had been halted by the United Automobile Workers' strike at eighty-eight plants and facilities where the union has eighty-five separate bargaining units. The Mahwah assembly plant was among those being struck.

On October 13, 1961, the United Automobile Workers ordered strikes against the Ford Motor Company ended with the exception of two plants, Walton Hills, OH and Wayne, MI. Local issues at these two plants were settled later.[58] The move was part of an effort to get the second largest auto maker back into production under a new three-year national economic package.[59]

Ford halts it assembly lines due to a strike at a stamping plant – June 15, 1962.

On June 6, 1962 a strike was called at the Walton Hills, Ohio stamping facility. Because of the strike and the shortage of sheet metal parts for cars that resulted, Ford halted car production in its sixteen assembly plants on June 15, 1962. The struck plant made body parts for all Ford cars except the Lincoln line. Truck production continued at some of the plants, including Mahwah, NJ.[60]

The strike at Walton Hills was the climax to a long period of disagreement over production standards, or work rates, on some forty jobs.

Ford Mahwah plant halted by walkout – November 27, 1962.

Production of passenger cars and trucks at the Ford plant in Mahwah stopped when 4,350 members of Local 906, United Automobile Workers, struck over 83 grievances. Negotiations had been underway, when a five-day strike notice expired. The grievances covered a variety of complaints under the headings of production and health safety, two of the three reasons that permit strikes under the three year contract that went into effect in October, 1961. The third reason was wage rates for new jobs.[61]

---

[57] New York Times, November 20, 1960, *Ford Strike Averted, pg. 82.*

[58] New York Times, October 16, 1961, *Ford Union to End All But 2 Strikes, pg. 23.*

[59] New York Times, October 4, 1961, *Bargaining Units in the Strike, pg. 37.*

[60] New York Times, June 16, 1962, *Ford Halts Its Assembly Lines in Strike at a Stamping Plant,* Damon Stetson, pg. 32.

[61] New York Times, November 28, 1962, *Ford Mahwah Plant Halted By Walkout, pg. 62.*

While small groups picketed at the gates of the plant when the walkout started at 9AM, there were no serious disturbances and 650 salaried employees entered the plant without incident.[62]

International Brotherhood of Teamsters / Car Haulers Strike – June 1964.

On June 22, 1964, the Teamsters went on strike against NuCar-Carriers and Automobile Transport Company, both of Mahwah. They normally transported vehicles made at the Ford plant to dealers. The strike began when the locals refused to accept a national contract offered by the haulers. It was reported that James A. Hoffa, president of the International Brotherhood of Teamsters, had backed the idea of such a contract. The locals were reported to have resisted it, fearing loss of their autonomy.

Cars were backed up at plant sites unable to be delivered. At Ford's Mahwah plant, the largest installation affected, 13,500 cars and trucks were grounded. On June 29, the Ford Motor Company obtained in Superior Court, Hackensack, NJ, a temporary restraint forbidding striking teamsters from interfering with the storing of new cars on leased property. Ford supervisory personnel tried to drive new vehicles to lease property, but were stopped by mass picketing. On July 6, Superior Court Judge Theodore I Botter delayed argument on an order requiring the International Brotherhood of Teamsters to show why it should not be permanently enjoined from stopping the Ford Motor Company from moving new cars from its Mahwah plant to nearby leased storage space.[63] The case was put off until August 6, 1964. On July 11, representatives of 18 locals of the International Brotherhood of Teamsters Union reached an agreement with the haulers of the new cars, settling the strike that had choked off deliveries from automobile plants along the East coast. The announcement of the new three-year contract came after a 28 hour bargaining session at a motel in North Bergen, NJ, between the locals, all members of the Eastern Teamsters conference, and the 15 haulers.[64]

On July 24, 1964, the Ford Company announced that it would undertake a mammoth car washing operation to wash the over 10,000 car that have been sitting since the beginning of the Teamsters strike. The operation used water pumped from a stone quarry and muscle power supplied by 20 college students. The company rigged U-shaped pipes and portable steam engines to pump the water from the stone quarry and spray it on the cars that went through in assembly line fashion. The college students then moved in for the soaping and swabbing and the makeshift rig applied the rinsing. Two one hundred foot basins caught the soapy water and filtered it back into the ground. The cars were on their way to dealers in two weeks.[65]

[62] New York Times, November 28, 1962, *Ford Mahwah Plant Halted By Walkout*, pg. 62.
[63] New York Times, June 30, 1964, *Ford Wins an Order Against Teamsters*, pg. 20.
[64] New York Times, July 12, 1964, *Pact Reached To End Car Delivery Strike*, Joseph Lelyveld, pg. 1.
[65] New York Times, July 25, 1964, *Ford Plant Preparing to Wash 10,000 Cars*, pg. 21.

Plant strikes cause slowdowns and layoffs – November, 1964.

Ford's production was cut by 75% as a result of strikes at 9 assembly plants and manufacturing plants on November 6, 1964. Negotiations had been in progress for five months. These nine plants were just the last to come to agreement and went on strike. Assembly plants that were still in operation were severely impacted by the lack of supplies from the manufacturing facilities. The plants involved in the strike actions were:

Dallas, TX – Assembly plant
Louisville, KY – Assembly plant
Buffalo, NY – Doors, roof panels, floor panels
Chicago, IL – Front fenders, hoods, instrument panels, floor pans
Ypsilanti, MI – Heaters, generators, alternators, brake cylinders, shock absorbers, starters
Sterling Township, MI – Rear axles, drive shafts
Wayne, MI – Assembly plant
Wayne, MI – Truck assembly plant
Sheffield, AL – Aluminum foundry

As a result of the action 80,000 workers had been affected, 25,000 who walked out and 55,000 who had been laid-off as a result of the shortages. About 3,000 workers at the Mahwah plant, almost the entire assembly line force were laid off. The Ford Motor Company and the United Automobile Workers signed a new three year contract on November 23, 1964, thus ending the strike and resuming parts production, permitting the assembly plants to re-open.

Workers furloughed because of the strike-caused parts shortage returned to work at the Mahwah assembly plant on November 27, 1964.[66] [67]

UAW strike against Ford impacts 160,000 workers in 25 states – September 6, 1967.

The Ford Motor Company was struck by the United Automobile Workers at midnight September 6, 1967, after the company rejected a union offer to submit their differences on pay and fringe benefits to binding arbitration. The strike idled about 160,000 Ford workers in 25 states earning $5.2 million a day in wages and halted Ford's production of about 10,000 cars and trucks a day.

Neither side would estimate how long the strike would last. Malcolm L. Denise, Ford's chief negotiator, who was also a company vice president, said that he would continue the talks with optimism, as he had begun the first bargaining sessions, and "see how long it takes to get it done." Walter P. Reuther, the union president, said that "the only fair way" to determine wages was by examining Ford's productivity. But the company refused to discuss this "and because of this we've got a strike."

---

[66] New York Times, November 14, 1964, *Ford Layoffs Rise Despite New Pact*, Damon Stetson, pg. 17.
[67] New York Times, November 24, 1964, *Ford and Union Sign 3-Year Pact*, pg. 33.

Henry Ford II, the company's chairman, called the strike "totally unjustified and completely unnecessary." "Because we would not accede to the unconscionable demands of a powerful union," he said," we are paying a stiff penalty." He said that employees, stockholders, dealers, customers, supplier companies "and millions of others are forced to suffer the consequences with us." "This is unjust and, in every sense of the word, tragic in its implications for the whole nation."

Mr. Reuther said that the union and the company were "completely deadlocked on the economics" – the size of the wages and fringe benefits increases in any new contract. He proposed that a three man panel decide the economic issues. Ford offered the union a three year contract with increases in pay and fringe benefits estimated at 55 to 60 cents an hour over three years or about a 4 percent increase per year. The union wanted at least 6 percent per year, or about 90 cents an hour over three years. Mr. Reuther, in turning down the company's offer said that the proposals on straight pay and pension increases fell far short of union demands. "A strike can be averted if you will join us in substituting the power of persuasion for the persuasion of power – if you will join with us in seeking resolution to the economic matters in dispute in a form of impartial judgment rather than through a contest of economic power," Mr. Reuther wrote in a letter to Ford.

Union officials also charged that the Big Three automobile companies – Ford, General Motors, and Chrysler corporation – were working together to break the unions "whipsaw" tactic of striking one car maker at a time. The last two were not affected by this strike.[68]

Although the Ford strike was not scheduled to begin until midnight, about 1,500 workers at a car assembly plant in St. Paul jumped the gun by walking off their jobs at 12:45PM.

At the Mahwah, NJ Ford assembly plant, 1,900 workers began walking off the job at 8:30PM and by 9:00PM the plant was closed. An official of Local 906 of the UAW said the men acted spontaneously and had not been directed by the union to walk off their jobs before the midnight deadline. The night shift came to work at 5:00PM and normally would have worked until 1:30AM. Some of those who walked out said management personnel goaded them after they went to work by asking them what time they planned to walk out. "My foreman asked me if I was working until midnight and I said yes," said one worker, "then he told me others had already started to leave, so I left too."[69]

In St. Louis, 1,300 workers walked off the job at 9:00PM.

November 6, 1967, new 1968 Fords began rolling off the assembly lines for the first time in two months. The United Auto Workers' strike against the Ford Motor Company finally ended on November 1, 1967 with the signing of a new three year contract, but local disputes delayed the

[68] New York Times, September 7, 1967, *Ford Strike is On a Company Bars Arbitration Bid*, pg. 1.
[69] New York Times, September 7, 1967, *Jersey Workers Walk Out Early*, Val Adams, pg. 26.

car line start-up. The first post strike Ford, a green Mustang, drove off the line at Dearborn, MI, at 6:35AM. The car had been sitting near the end of the line, all but complete, when the strike began.

Three Ford assembly operations resumed on November 6, 1967 – the car plant at Dearborn and truck lines at plants in Mahwah, NJ and San Jose, CA. All the other plants resumed operations within the next few days with the exception of Dallas, TX; Lorain, OH; St. Louis, MO; and Wixom, MI due to some local agreements yet to be worked out.

United Black Workers shut down Mahwah plant operations, April 27, 1969.

About 500 black workers protesting racism stayed off the job and forced the closing of the Mahwah plant. Workers were sent home after the 4:00PM shift began, and the assembly lines came to a halt.

The walkout was called by the United Black Brotherhood of Ford Mahwah after a black worker charged that a supervisor had insulted him with a racial epithet.

After the foreman was removed and the wildcat strike ended, the United Black Workers of Ford Mahwah was organized. It maintained relations with the League of Revolutionary Black Workers, an organization of black workers' caucuses at automobile plants in the Detroit area.[70]

Wilbur Haddock, one of the organizers, spoke in an interview about organizing at the Ford plant, in Mahwah, NJ. He said that after initial successes, they had put on black leather jackets and decked themselves out in pins and badges. Their support seemed to fade rather than develop. One day, he pulled aside an older worker he trusted and asked what the problem was. He was told that the workers were now scared of the organizers. They are not talking and walking as they had when the organizing had begun. The man said, "Now you're some kind of commando, but I'm just a Ford worker like I always was." Haddock hastened to add that it was not the political perspective that was upsetting workers, but the costuming, which suggested some kind of action more designed for mass media consumption than for defeating the company.

District 65, a United Automobile Workers affiliate since 1981, became a full-fledged department of the international union on April 27, 1969 and led a UAW campaign to enlist white-collar workers across the nation.

The president of the UAW, Owen F. Bieber, and the president of District 65, David Livingston, announced the agreement at District 65's headquarters at 13 Astor Place in Manhattan.

---

[70] New York Times, April 29, 1969, *Ford Plant Shut in Racial Dispute*, Walter H. Waggoner, pg. 23.

Figure 54 - Joseph Reilly, president of Local 906, addresses a rally outside union headquarters.

"We have operated well together for the past six years on the basis of a relatively unstructured affiliation," Mr. Beiber said, "now we will operate even more effectively on the basis of organic unity."

Started in 1933 by dry goods workers on Manhattan's Lower East Side, District 65 expanded into a variety of industries, both in manufacturing and retail trade, and since the early 1970's has been a leader in organizing workers in technical, office and professional fields. By integrating District 65 into its organization, the UAW hopes to increase its strength in these areas. "We're trying to strengthen the structure of the UAW to bring more people in," Mr. Beiber said. 'They Can Use Our Expertise'

"We can use their influence, their financial strength and their political clout," Mr. Livingston said, "and they can use our expertise in the white-collar area."

The Plant Closing

Driving Forces

After 25 years, on June 20, 1980, the Ford Motor Company's plant at Mahwah, NJ closed.

When Ford Motor Company executives began weighing their choices of plants to shut down in the company's drive to reduce its mounting losses, they looked most closely at the quality of work in their many factories, and the Mahwah plant, they said, headed the list of facilities with evidence of poor workmanship.

Although the auto workers' union disputed the company's conclusion, the problem of poor quality in the Ford Fairmonts and Mercury Zephyrs assembled in Mahwah emerged as the principle reason for closing the plant.

Answering the question on "what was wrong" with the Mahwah plant to force its closing, Harold A. Poling, Fords executive vice president for North American operations, said, "In comparison with other facilities, their quality reputation, as demonstrated by the repairs per hundred and one month service costs, was not as good as the others." Mr. Poling added that the cost comparisons with the other plants making the two mid-sized cars also showed that the Mahwah plant was more costly to run per car produced than the two others.[71]

Arvid Jouppi, a Detroit based automotive analyst, was somewhat surprised that Mahwah was a victim of Ford's retrenchment. "The plant and its work force had a good reputation," he said, "but one big disadvantage was the increasing cost of shipping components to Mahwah from factories in the Midwest".

The president of the Mahwah local of the United Auto Workers, Joseph P. O'Hara, acknowledged there had been problems with workmanship in the past, but maintained they had been largely corrected. "Over the last year, we have met with top management at Mahwah and they have stated clearly that quality has improved 100 percent," he said' "Mahwah builds the best quality unit in the country."

The plant closed amid management and union bickering about the quality of Fords made there, slumping sales and profits, the company's misreading of the American car buyers current tastes, and bitterness and anxiety about the growing presence of Japanese cars on the market.

Auto industry observers believe that Ford's delay in producing versions of cars then in heavy demand was the key factor in the economic slumps.

---

[71] New York Times, April 17, 1980, *Quality of Work at Mahwah Cited by Ford as Factor in Plant*

The Last Car off the Line

As disconsolate workers walked out of the Ford Motor Company's assembly plant for the last time, the company closed its doors, eliminating 4500 jobs.

The closing, amid demands from both company and union officials for steps to limit the import of Japanese-made cars, ended 50 years of Ford manufacturing in Bergen County, NJ. In the first 25 years in Bergen County, Ford produced cars in a plant in Edgewater, over the next 25 years, the company cars and trucks at its 50 acre plant in Mahwah.

Including Mahwah, nine major automobile plants had been permanently closed across the nation in the year spanning June, 1979 to June, 1980, with 15,000 workers losing their jobs.

"I feel sad about America's future," Bill Cunningham, a shop steward, said after driving the last car - the plant's 4,594,234th – off the assembly line. It was a two-tone beige Futura, destined for a dealership in West Frankfurt, IL. "Cars are the backbone of the economy," Mr. Cunninham said, "We're in trouble."

Figure 55 - The last car from the Mahwah plant rolls down the line.

Ben Spinnelli, who transferred to Mahwah when the Edgewater plant closed 25 years earlier, placed a small American flag on the windshield of the last car. "This is an American plant, built by Americans, and American cars should be coming out of it," he said, referring to Ford's willingness to accept purchase offers for the plant from foreign competitors. "We'll gear up for the small car. Ford got caught short, but we'll catch up."

Figure 56 - An American flag is placed on the windshield by Ben Spinelli.

Figure 57 - Workers bid the last car farewell.

Figure 58 - The last car leaving the plant.

As for his future, Mr. Spinnelli, a 44 year old resident of Jersey City, said: "I'm going to hang in awhile and collect my benefits. After a year, I'll have to see what I can do. I'll have to train myself all over again for something new."

However, the mood on the Mahwah assembly line on the last day was not all gloomy. Hundreds of executives and workers thronged along the end of the line. The workers cheered as Mr. Cunningham drove off the last car. Then workers gathered a last time to do some back slapping and hand shaking.[72]

Aid for Workers

New Jersey's Department of Labor and Industry, which opened a job-referral and job retraining center in the headquarters of the United Auto Workers, Local 906 near the plant, stated that the plant shutdown had affected 4,148 union employees, including 3,346 who were dismissed the day the plant closed and 802 left temporarily jobless when the production of pick-up trucks halted the previous July. In addition 425 Ford management officials were left jobless.

The homes of the unionized workers were scattered throughout the metropolitan area. There were 2,301 in New Jersey, including 824 in Bergen County and 400 in Passaic County. A total of 1,816 lived in New York State.

---

[72] New York Times, June 21, 1980, *Last Ford Leaves Mahwah Plant; 4500 Employees Lose Their Jobs*, Robert Hanley, pg. 1.

The loss of weekly salaries would be cushioned for a while by a combination of state, Federal and union-management funds. For up to 52 weeks, the dismissed workers were entitled to 95 percent of each week's pay from a combination of state unemployment compensation; management-union supplemental unemployment benefits, and readjustment allowances under the Federal Trade Assistance Act of 1974, which insured financial assistance for workers who lose their jobs because of foreign imports. Annual salaries for most unionized workers ranged from $15,000 to $20,000.

Personal Hardships

Cynthia Anderson, who for seven years has overseen the installation of seat belts and back windows on the assembly line, figured she would break the news to her two children by showing them the company's letter of explanation. When leaving for the day, as she opened her car door, several men from the plant called out: "Hey Anderson. Now that your contract with Ford is up, do you think Hollywood will give you one?" "I think so," she said with a laugh.[73]

John Hendricks, an installer of brackets on mufflers and tailpipes, said he was worried about meeting the monthly mortgage and tax payments of $350 on his home in Waldwick. "And my food bills – they're driving me up the wall," said the 44-year-old father of three children, aged 13 to 17.

Bob Berner, a 48 year old inventory clerk who came to Mahwah from Edgewater and put in 25 years with Ford, turned out for the last day's work in a black T-shirt with white lettering saying: "Buy Foreign Peanuts." "I don't want to put President Carter's peanut farm out of business," he said referring to his shirt's admonition. "I just want to make him hungry like we're going to be." Mr. Brener's thoughts were that he hoped he could support his family for a year on the compensation he received from Ford, the union and the state government. "Then I'll learn how to repair air-conditioners and refrigerators."

A survey conducted in the Fall of 1981, more than a year after the plant closing, indicated that large numbers of the Mahwah Ford plant workers remained jobless: 55.8 percent of those who responded said that they were still unemployed. This did not include those who retired or who were not looking for a job.

Age was against many of the laid off workers. In December 1981, Ben Szachiewicz, who at the time was 55, completed a computer repair course paid for by Federal job-training funds. He said employers were looking for people who would be with them 5, 10, 15 years down the road.

For the first time in 34 years, Eugene Pfeiffer, an ex-plant utility man, could not find a job. "I've been working since I was 12," he said. "It gives a man a very disgusted feeling to know that

---

[73] The Record, April 16, 1980, *Workers Stunned by Closing at Ford*, Mary Schwarz and Ann Rauma.

you're out there looking, and its closed doors no matter where you go." "When you are working, you have more respect from the family," he said, "all of a sudden I feel like a piece of furniture around the house." [74]

---

[74] New York Times, April 25, 1982, *Majority from Ford's Mahwah Plant Still Jobless*, pg. 56.

Plant Demolition

After several attempts they were unable to find a buyer for the empty assembly plant. The land on which it sat was desired more than the plant itself. It was the winter of 1984, almost 30 years to the day after the plant's doors were first opened, dump trucks, bulldozers and wrecking cranes arrived, and debris from the factory that once epitomized what Henry Luce would call the American Century was crushed and dumped as landfill into the New Jersey's Meadowlands.

Figure 59 - the plant is demolished.

After Ford

The Ford plant was an important part of the history of Mahwah. Its closing led to a period of uncertainty and how the void would be filled. When the Ford plant opened, Mahwah was on the brink of a transition. The fear was that transition had come to a sudden halt. However, this was not the case. Businesses and industries again flourished and the growth in Mahwah continued.

Sharp Electronics

In 1984, Sharp Corporation of Japan bought 65 acres of the north end of the Ford property. Plans called for the Ford plant to be demolished and construction started by the end of 1984

Figure 60 - The new Sharp Corporate Headquarters in the distance, remnants of the Ford plant in the foreground.

Photo – Tom O'Brien

Figure 61 - Sharp Corporate Headquarters.

In March, 1986, Japan's Sharp Corp. opened a 500.000 square foot U.S. headquarters. The building would house a 150,000 square foot headquarters building and a 350,000 square foot service and distribution facility.[75] Unlike the Ford plant Sharp's new building is quiet, and the landscaping has replaced the asphalt fields that surrounded the Ford plant.

Sheraton Mahwah Hotel

In 1984, New Jersey Developer, J.D. Construction Co. paid $120,000 an acre for the land on which it was preparing to build a hotel plus office space for 7,000 people.[76] Although the original plan called for further expansion beyond the hotel, this did not happen. The Sheraton Mahwah Hotel has become a landmark site in Mahwah. Remnants of the Ford plant's foundation can still be seen in the area of the hotel. The railroad yard and spurs have been removed and is now a popular spot for walkers.

From the old industrial environment, with all the noise, smells, and chaotic movement, to the more serene atmosphere at the site today, this corner of Mahwah has undergone a significant transformation.

Photo – Tom O'Brien

Figure 62 - Sheraton Mahwah Hotel.

[75] New York Times, November 25, 1984, *Sharp Taking Part of Ford Plant Site*
[76] ibid

Edgewater

Even the site of the old Edgewater plant has found new life. Built on the original foundation of the old plant, a modern, luxury, condominium complex has been built.

Photo – Tom O'Brien

Figure 63 - Independence Harbor, Edgewater, NJ, built on the site of the old Ford plant building foundation.

Lingering Problems

Beside the unemployment that impacted many of the Ford employees long after the plant closing, the effect of waste dumped in the surrounding area and sometimes beyond has left its mark on the environment in terms of pollution. The effects of the sludge consisting of paint, oils, solvents, lacquer, etc. deposited in various dumps and abandoned mines may never be fully understood. Follow-on studies have produced evidence citing contaminated drinking water, wildlife, and soil, human illness and death that can be strongly attributed to the wanton and careless dumping practices. It is a problem stemming from the existence of the industrial facilities, such as the Ford plant, that we will have to contend with well into the future.

References

Bibliography

New York Times, May 6, 1953, *Ford Getting Site for Jersey Plant.*

New York Times, August 12, 1953, *Ford Gets Jersey Site.*

Ramsey Journal, August 13, 1953, *Ford Signs Contract With Erie.*

Ramsey Journal, September 3, 1953, *New Erie Spur Track Construction in High Gear.*

Ramsey Journal, December 31, 1953, *Photo – Aerial View of the Proposed Site (Ford Motor Co.).*

Ramsey Journal, February 25, 1954, *Photo – Structural steel erections for the new Ford Plant.*

Ramsey Journal, May 20, 1954, *Photo – Crane lifting wall panel into place at Ford plant.*

Ramsey Journal, May 6, 1954, *Will the Ford Plant Affect Us.*

New York Times, June 10, 1954, *Ford in Power Contract*

Ramsey Journal, December 30, 1954, *Ford Tells How Mahwah Site was Selected.*

New York Times, June 6, 1955, *Pickets Appear at Some Plants.*

New York Times, June 7, 1955, *37 of 68 Plants Closed by Strikes*

New York Times, June 25, 1955, *Ford Shows Off Mahwah Plant, Big Enough for 7 Football Fields.*

Ramsey Journal, July 14, 1955, *Ford's Move from Edgewater to New Mahwah Plant Starts Today Production to Begin on Tuesday.*

New York Times, July 16, 1955, *Ford Plant Closes at Edgewater with 1,817,938th Car in 25 Years.*

New York Times, July 17, 1955, *First Ford Rolls in Mahwah Plant.*

New York Times, July 19, 1955, *Auto for Crippled Given to Institute.*

Ramsey Journal, July 21, 1955, *Mahwah Ford Plant Covers 177 Acres.*

Ramsey Journal, July 28, 1955, *New Mahwah Ford plant is a Miracle of Modern Planning and Design.*

Mahwah Star, September 30, 1955, *Confidence in Future Economy of America Cited by Henry Ford*

Mahwah Star, September 30, 1955, *14,000 at Ford Dedication; Firm Investing Half-Billion on Expansion*

Ramsey Journal, September 30, 1955, *Ford is Staking $500,000,000 in 1956 on Prosperity of U.S.*

New York Times, October 6, 1955, *Ford Plant to add Shift*

Erie Magazine, November, 1955, *Huge Mahwah Ford Plant Opens*

New York Times, December 23, 1955, *Ford Adding 2D Shift*

Ridgewood Herald News, August 2, 1956, *Ford Organizes Fire Brigades in Plant*

New York Times, December 11, 1957, *Ford Strike is Voted.*

Ramsey Journal, April 10, 1958, *Photo – Fire at the Ford Motor Company Assembly Plant in Mahwah*

New York Times, October 24, 1958, *Jersey Ford Plant Reassembles One of 15,000,000*

Ramsey Journal, July 9, 1959, *Safety Assured at Ford Plant by Work of 2 Men Using Many Different Kinds of Equipment.*

New York Times, January 31, 1960, *6 Held in Looting at Ford Factory.*

New York Times, March 9, 1960, *Ford Gets Army Work.*

New York Times, November 20, 1960, *Ford Strike Averted.*

New York Times, September 8, 1961, *Plant in New Jersey is Sold by Ford*

New York Times, June 21, 1980, *Last Ford Leaves Mahwah Plant; 4500 Employees Lose Their Jobs*

New York Times, October 4, 1961, *Bargaining Units in the Strike*

New York Times, October 16, 1961, *Ford Union to End All But 2 Strikes*

New York Times, April 22, 1962, *Plant Gives Inside Look to Visitors*

New York Times, June 16, 1962, *Ford Halts Its Assembly Lines in Strike at a Stamping Plant*

The Evening News, 1962, *Ford Mahwah Plant, a City that Never Sleeps.*

New York Times, November 28, 1962, *Ford Mahwah Plant Halted By Walkout*

New York Times, April 15, 1963, *Ford Shares in Contract*

New York Times, June 30, 1964, *Ford Wins an Order Against Teamsters*

New York Times, July 4, 1964, *New Car Abound But Buyers Wait*

New York Times, July 7, 1964, *Hearing Delayed in Jersey on Ford-Teamster Fight*

New York Times, July 12, 1964, *Pact Reached To End Car Delivery Strike.*

New York Times, July 12, 1964, *Industry Begins Plant Closings*

New York Times, July 25, 1964, *Ford Plant Preparing to Wash 10,000 Cars*

New York Times, November 14, 1964, *Ford Layoffs Rise Despite New Pact*

New York Times, November 24, 1964, *Ford and Union Sign 3-Year Pact*

New York Times, November 28, 1964, *Ford Plants Back to Work at Mahwah and Metuchen*

The Journal, July 16, 1965, *Ford Plant Celebrates 10th Year*

New York Times, September 7, 1967, *Ford Strike is On a Company Bars Arbitration Bid*

New York Times, September 7, 1967, *Jersey Workers Walk Out Early*

New York Times, November 7, 1967, *Production at Ford, Halted Two Months by Strike, Resumes*

New York Times, August 10, 1968, *Ford Recalls 14,600 Trucks for Possible Safety Defect*

Home and Store News, August 21, 1968, *Ford Plant is in Changeover*

New York Times, April 29, 1969, *Ford Plant Shut in Racial Dispute*

New York Times, April 30, 1969, *Negroes at Ford's Jersey Plant Continue Strike*

Home and Store News, August 24, 1977, *Ford Plant Open for Tours*

Home and Store News, November 11, 1977, *Mahwah Ford has Plant Tours*

The Reporter, June 29, 1978, *Ford Gala Honors Workers.*

The Record, April 16, 1980, *Closing of Mahwah Ford plant to idle 3,732*

The Record, April 16, 1980, *Workers Stunned by Closing at Ford,* Mary Schwarz and Ann Rauma.

New York Times, April 17, 1980, *Quality of Work at Mahwah Cited by Ford as Factor in Plant Closing*

New York Times, May 5, 1980, *Kennedy Says Carter Fiscal Policy Doomed Auto Plant in New Jersey*

New York Times, May 11, 1980, *Exercise in Futility*

New York Times, June 21, 1980, *Last Ford Leaves Mahwah Plant; 4,500 Employees Lose Their Jobs*

New York Times, April 25, 1982, *Majority from Ford's Mahwah Plant Still Jobless*

New York Times, November 25, 1984, *Sharp Taking Part of Ford Plant site*

Forbes, May 5, 1986, *Mahwah,* John Merwin.

The Record, March 10, 2008, *Making a Wasteland: Ford, the Feds, the Mob*

Websites

www.loveFords.com

www.wikipedia.com

www.history.com

www.Ford.com

www.nytimes.com

www.northjersey.com

www.corpwatch.org

Index